The Art of Blogging:
The Inside Tips and Tricks
On how to dominate it

I0511259

By Ted Dawson

Table of Contents

Introduction

Ten years ago when Mathew was browsing Google, he realized that there were many people like him who were clueless about weight loss techniques. Mathew was passionate about fitness and weight loss. He read a lot of books on fitness, tried all kinds of diets and gymmed to lose weight. He saw that there were websites and ebooks available, but they requested payment to be downloaded. That is when he decided to start a blog on fitness and weight loss. He bought a domain name and registered with a host who offered him blog space. He penned his thoughts on diet foods and wrote his experiences with fitness. Initially he sent emails to his friends about his blog and they visited. In three month's time Mathew had published around 25 blog posts with attractive pictures and videos. He saw that by then there were comments under many of his posts. That encouraged him to publish more blog posts. That is how Mathew became a blogger.

Around that time Google had come up with keyword search and search engine optimization (SEO). Mathew learnt all about it and decided to follow SEO tactics to get more traffic. Those were the days when article directories were very popular. Getting back links from article directories helped in improving search rank. Mathew visited a freelance marketing place and got 1000 articles written about fitness and weight loss. He hired freelancers to do the content writing. He posted each of the articles in popular directories like Ezine and got back links from each of them. In those days there were around 500 article directories online.

As a next step he got an ebook ghostwritten about fitness & weight loss and put it for sale on Clickbank.com and Commission Junction. These were extremely popular websites (ten years ago) to sell digital products. The affiliates on Click Bank picked up his ebook to promote on their landing pages. Mathew received another 145 back links thanks to affiliates. He also sold the ebook through his blog. He gave a 5 page free download on his blog for a sign in. Seeing traffic and footfalls to his blog, Google started posting ads on his blog. These were relevant to his blog subject (fitness & weight loss).

Since it is free to become an affiliate on Click Bank, Mathew became one and started promoting other's products besides his. He promoted them through his blog. By 2008 social media grew and Facebook became a place to promote products. Mathew started a Facebook page and joined forums to create awareness for his blog. He also promoted weight loss products like Weight Watchers and Nutrisystem on his blog. Every time someone bought these products Mathew received a commission.

As the internet evolved so did Mathew's blog. He made his blog into a vibrant place where people could communicate with him directly as well as publish guest posts. Every time someone posted a guest post, Mathew was paid for it as well as he received a back link. Mathew had a buzzing blog with an excellent Page rank 7 and Alexa rating (>500). He was earning around $2000 per month through selling his ebook, affiliate marketing, publishing guest posts for a fee and Google Adwords program. He also sold diets, fitness equipments and offered discount coupons on his blog. From being a passive earner his blog became a primary revenue generator for Mathew.

As luck would have it, was around this time that Google changed its search criterion. The article directories went out of style and landing pages were black listed by Google. All the effort Mathew had put in till then had to be changed. This was in the year 2012. Amazon and Kindle were becoming a buzzing place to sell ebooks and Mathew jumped on to the bandwagon. With Social media in full force he promoted his blog through Facebook, Twitter and Instagram. He gave direct links from his blog to his social media pages and vice versa. He had his own diet channel on YouTube and drove traffic from there too.

After ten exciting years, Mathew today has a million followers and one small tweet from him, fetches a fortune as he's considered to be the fitness expert online. His videos on diet and weight loss are watched by more than a million viewers around the globe. There are diets and T-shirts under his name and his protein shakes and weight loss supplements are a rage among users. Yet Mathew continues to update his blog every two days with videos, latest information and products.

Today Mathew's net worth is two million dollars thanks to his humble blog that started as a passion ten years ago.

It is important to learn here that passion and vocation can be combined to make a successful career. Once you learn the ropes of blogging it'll be easy to optimize and monetize it. All you need is zest and zeal to pursue your passion.

Today it's free to start a blog. You no longer need to pay to maintain a blog. Thanks to Google and WordPress, blog space is freely available. Even the themes and look of your blog are available off the rack. You don't need to pay a web designer to start a blog. Go online, choose your niche, download a theme for free and start blogging.

Chapter 1 - What is a blog?

A blog is ideally a web page or website where you update regularly. It is maintained by an individual or a small group of members. It is informal and conversational in style. Right from the Prime Minister of a country to a businessman, musician, writer, actor and common man anybody and everybody can have a blog. It connects you directly to the readers and your message gets passed on instantly.

You can set free your imaginative powers on your blog updates. Blogging is an excellent marketing tool. You can instantly promote your company to buyers and create awareness about your latest products. People reading your blog will know what sort of a person you are through your posts. The pleasure you gain in publishing a blog post may be quite different from writing with a pen on paper. But the pounding on the keyboard helps you to unleash your creativity and make your thoughts known to people all around the world.

Content is the king here. When you start a blog you should be clear about why you've started it, what is it you wish to share and how to make the content interesting. Once you've addressed these three issues, your blog is sure to be a success. Don't blog to earn money. As a blogger, be passionate to share your knowledge with the world. That'll help you to earn money. Though you need to keep in mind about search engine optimization and keywords, don't stuff it to make your blog look like a software code. Write for human consumption and not for search engines.

Be humorous while writing blog posts. That'll attract readers. Your posts don't need to be dry and dull. Even if you're blogging about divorce make it interesting and allow readers to participate in the conversation. That'll increase the traffic. Also visit other blogs and post comments. Reply to comments on your blog posts. That'll endear you to the reader.

History of blogging

It is believed that in 1994 Justin Hall, a college student created Links.net as his web page which later on in 1997 came to be known as 'Weblog' by Jorn Barger. In 1999 Peter Merholz broke the phrase and made it 'we blog' on his side bar which shortly came to be known as 'blog'. In a blog, posts are posted in reverse, the latest ones being on the top/ main page for everyone to see.

After a while, Evan Williams of Pyra Labs used the term blog as both noun and verb and coined the term 'blogger'. These terms became popular and spread like wild fire all over the net. Initially people were only able to post articles and posts in text. Later images, audios and videos came along and today a blog is vibrant and buzzing with activity.

From being a socially acclaimed past time, blogging took a serious turn when search engines like Google made it possible for bloggers to monetize on them. That brought in writers and bloggers who wished to make money online. Ten years ago when there was a global meltdown, thousands of people lost their jobs; it was blogs and the internet that helped people survive by making money online. Blogs became a source of passive income and today have come a long way and made millionaires and billionaires.

Chapter 2 - How a blog Works

Blog is a web journal where usually a single author pens his thoughts and opinions about a certain topic. A blog works both from the front end and back end. To put it in simple words, front end is the design of the blog page, what the reader sees, and back end is where the programming is done. Basically it is web design and web development that is also known as front end and back end. A person working on the front end is known as a web designer. This person decides the layout for the blog and what text to add, html, etc. This person doesn't touch the code. They use software's like Photoshop, Fireworks to create web pages/ blogs. A web designer is only a visual designer who focuses on the way the blog looks. As there are readymade themes available, the web designer may simply buy them and make some changes to suit a blogger's needs.

The work done in the back end is known as web development. The work is done on the insides of a blog from the server side. You can't see the work   as it is in the servers and databases. Back end work is very important for a dynamic blog as it gets updated regularly, that too in real time. This programming is done in languages like PHP and or .Net. A person who knows both front and back end can always work as a web designer and developer and handle both the jobs with aplomb. A complete grasp of programming is a must to be successful in both front and back end.

This will help the blog to get updated smoothly without any hitch. Uploading of images, videos and other media will be done smoothly if there is harmony between front and back ends.

Tips to blog successfully

If you are interested in blogging successfully, then the following tips will help you immensely:

Always provide the best quality when you write your blogs. Good readers always appreciate it. You will also need to see to it that your writing quality doesn't go down when you blog regularly.

Don't keep changing your URL when you are regularly writing your blogs. Your regular readers will prefer if you write in the same URL.

Choose the topics of your blogs wisely. Write on topics which will appeal to a large group of readers.

If you are writing on a blog topic which needs technical knowhow, see to it that you acquire it before you write your blog.

The more research you do for your blog, the better it will appear to your readers. Don't avoid doing research if your blog topic deserves it.

You should always have a bit of patience when you write a blog. Only if you keep coming with interesting topics for your blogs will your readers keep coming back for more. For this, you need to devote some time and patience.

You should love writing or sharing your experiences if you want to be a successful blogger. Don't try to be conscious when you write your blog.

You also need to market your blogs successfully after you write them. You can start with your list of friends on various social forums for the same.

You might need to devote time exclusively for your blogging activity. This is because you should always try to be one up over other bloggers if you want to be unique on the web.

Always feel free to take tips from other bloggers who have been writing for a long time. Their experiences will help you to gain useful inputs on blogging.

How to Choose the Correct Platform for Your Blog

Choosing the correct platform for your blog is very important as all your hard work in planning, creating and writing your blog will go to waste if you don't choose the right platform for your blog. Very often many bloggers try to blindly follow what the other bloggers are doing. That's a grave mistake they are making as what might work for some bloggers might not work for other bloggers.

Each blogger has his or her uniqueness connected with a blog. So it's not right to blindly club all the blogs in the same bracket. Try to use a platform which will effectively utilize a neat combination of the program you use and interface which will put your blog across to your readers.

If you use a highly customized program, it will turn to be more troublesome to use. In case you are not very comfortable with the fundamentals of html and other web languages, take the help of a well qualified web designer to create the right platform for your blog.

Some of the platforms which can be used by you: blogger, WordPress, nucleus, Joomla, etc. You need to zoom in on the platform which serves your purpose in the best possible way. Try to know what are the positives and negatives of each platform before you actually choose one for your own blog. WordPress is one of the handy platforms which are used by a large number of bloggers on the internet.

Finally you also have the option of using the free hosting method or the self-hosting method for your blog. Once again each of these methods has their positives and negatives. You need to decide what will work well in your case. A free hosted blog is very easy to set up as it is done by the blog host. You will also find the posting part to be very easy. And as the name suggest, it doesn't cost you anything, so you don't need any money for hosting it. On the other hand a self hosted blog will help you to choose your own design for the blog as well as use a domain name of your choice. Besides this you can also make it as SEO friendly as you want it to be. But you would have to pay for the whole process. So you have to decide if you want to spend a bit and be independent or choose the free hosting option for your blog. It shouldn't be that your blog takes a long time to download or your data is missing. Your host should be fast, reliable and secure.

Is Blogging Right for You?

The following questions will help you to know if you have the right traits to be a blogger.

Are you good at managing time? Only if you are good at it can you regularly pay proper attention to all your blogs. You will also need the time to keep updating your knowledge of various topics.

Do you get affected very easily by what is said by others? Your answer should be a no, as you will be criticized very often by your readers on what you have written. The comments written by them might pass all levels of decency. So it's very important to face criticism without getting affected in a negative manner.

Are you good in conveying a message? Every blog tries to convey or communicate something to its target group or audience. If you are not very effective in getting your message across, then blogging is not your cup of tea.

Do you love to write? If your answer is a no, then blogging is not meant for you.

Are you independent by nature? You need to be totally independent as you will have to take a lot of decisions and get things started when you are starting a blog.

Do you have a strong sense of discipline? This is important; as you will regularly need to keep in touch with your readers, check their comments as well as take good care so that your blogs grow better week after week. You can achieve this only if you are disciplined by nature.

Do you enjoy being in the spotlight? Being a blogger means being always in the eyes of the public. You will not enjoy any kind of privacy once you start writing about your personal experiences and other aspects of life. Only if you can handle this should you trying blogging online.

Do you have a sense of humor? This is a much needed quality in bloggers. You will need to laugh at yourself at times while writing about yourself. If you have this quality, then you can definitely go ahead with blogging.

Do you like to interact with people? Interacting with people is an important part of Blogging. If you are good at it, then you will do well as a blogger.

Do you like to read? Reading is a very important quality which is needed in all bloggers. Only when you will read other blogs, comments, magazines, newspapers and other mediums can you grow as a blogger.

Chapter 3 - Choose your niche

Web log was found in 1997 by Jim Barger. It was like a dairy maintained on the internet to log in all your day's activities. You could update it and also sustain a personal touch. Web log got joined and became 'we blog' which later on came to be known as blog. The reason for blogs becoming popular was it gave people a platform to voice their opinions. Anybody can start a blog and this social media platform took a different turn to promote and market businesses as well.

Before you start a blog ask yourself what is it that you wish to share with readers. Why are you starting a blog? Is it to make money? Once these questions are answered then you can choose your niche. Often people start a blog because it's free and then after a few months their heart is not into it and it dies a quiet death. On other instance you start a blog about a subject you're not passionate about. Just because your friend spoke about it you started a blog. After the initial euphoria your writing was drab as you're not an expert on the subject. You lose interest and so does the reader.

First and foremost choose a niche for your blog that is interesting, will fetch you money as well as is your favorite subject. These three points matter to have a successful blog. Your posts should be about problem solving techniques. That is what will interest the reader. Ninety percent of people who browse the internet are looking for information regarding solutions to their problems.

Gardening

For example, Nikki's rose plant was infected with fungus making the buds dry. Nikki went online and looked for solutions to this problem. She found the solution on a gardening blog and immediately washed the plant with warm water and sprayed a medicinal liquid. Within a week the fungus was gone and the buds started to bloom.

Technical Solutions

If you're a technical person then your blog can offer technical solutions. Simple glitches that occur in your mobile or how to get rid of virus from your website are issues that can be discussed in your blog posts. You can also offer step by step images/ videos on how to set up software for your computer or other technical problems.

Fitness and weight loss

In case you're a health expert, offer homemade solutions to minor issues like aches and pains that occur during a workout session. These solutions should be holistic and not affect a person. Be responsible and serious about what advice you give. After all people are going to read and try them out. Be conscientious and truthful. A fitness blog can help obese people shed the extra flab. At the same time you can also sell fitness equipment on your blog. Diet coupons and discounts will endear readers to you. This is how you start a conversation with readers. Also it'll fetch you some money. Promoting a gym or product will get you income. Review products in all honesty.

Travel

Travel is one niche that is loved by all. Writing about places you've visited or about to visit will educate readers about various tourist attractions. Write about the weather, food habits, sights to see and what to wear to visit a particular place and see the response you get. People are looking for such information on the internet. You can also talk about cheap hotels, home stays, bed and breakfast, etc. Hotels and inns are looking for advertising online to attract customers. Big websites like Trip Advisor charge a high fee to promote small inns. If you've a fairly decent traffic you can earn a few bucks reviewing small inns and budget hotels.

Money

Money is what makes the world go around. Your blog can talk about how to save money, boost credit score, credit repair, debt consolidation and several other related issues that are plaguing the society. Give honest and sincere tips so that the reader believes you. Robert Smith had poor credit history due to over use of credit cards. He got an 'add on' card from his brother to boost his credit score. His brother's healthy credit history reflected on his report and boosted his credit score. He paid his utility bills on time and in six months time he was eligible for independent credit. He shared this information on his blog and informed readers that he's ready to help people boost their score for a fee. Several people consulted him and Robert became an expert in credit repair. He joined Google Adsense program and many lending institutions advertised on his blog and he made money through PPC (pay per click). He also wrote an ebook on credit repair and sold it on his blog as well on Kindle. Robert's blog established him as a credit repair expert.

Yoga and meditation

Holistic healing practices like yoga and meditation are extremely popular online. If you're a self help expert then your blog can have pictures and videos of asanas and meditation techniques. Yoga and meditation are the most searched keywords on Google.

Automobile

Who wouldn't be crazy about a mean machine? If you're passionate about cars then your blog can be about them. Car manufacturers are always looking for opportunities to sell. Advertise and review the cars and get paid for it. In case someone from your blog moves to the manufacturer's website then you'll be financially rewarded.

Whatever you do choose a niche you're passionate about.

How blogging helped a student get full scholarship in a top university

When Sonia was in high school she had a penchant for serving the less privileged kids. She volunteered at a neighborhood school for non-hearing kids and taught them dance. Yeah! She taught dance to kids who could not hear. With the help of rhythm and beat she timed their steps and made them swing to latest numbers. The children enjoyed it and loved her. She started a blog and shared her experiences of teaching them and how she learnt from them about sign language and their medium of communication. When she applied to universities for under graduate course in psychology she sent her blog address to all universities stating that she wishes to study about the language in which non-hearing kids think?

Her blog was thought provoking and interesting and unique. Her language was par excellence and she was awarded full scholarship of $120,000 by a well known university in USA.

This clearly shows that a blog can indeed help you to gain in many ways.

How to grow your blog

Now that you've started a blog, here comes the litmus test. It's not enough if you only start a blog. You need to publish posts and update your blog regularly. The information has to be recent, authentic and truthful. Don't simply copy, paste from other web sites or web magazines. The posts should be pertaining to your niche and you must have first hand information. This will attract traffic to your blog.

There are other ways to grow your blog. Write and publish guest posts in other blogs that are extremely popular in your niche. That'll help to identify you as an expert in your niche. Comment on other similar blogs and give a link to your blog. Invite other bloggers to visit your blog and publish posts. That'll help to grow your blog as well as traffic.

Well it's not that difficult to make your blogs grow if you write your posts by keeping the following tips in your mind when you write them:

It's very important to boost your readers. They are the ones who make your posts popular. So the next time if a reader writes a very interesting comment below your post, try to place that comment at the ending of your post. People love controversy so if you have it in you to write on controversial topics, then definitely go ahead and write on such topics. You will be able to generate a good response for the same.

Always write with lots of passion. Readers get drawn to blogs which are full of life. On the other hand, they avoid blogs which are dry in content. Try to have a proper sequence for your posts. Target a particular topic and continue writing on the same every week. Thus your readers will look forward to your post every week. You can develop a chain of posts which cover the same topic or interest but which keeps giving new aspects on it every week.

The more you cover topics which are hot and not written by anyone, better are your chances of doing well. So try to look for that rare nugget of news which will first feature on your post. This will definitely help you to carve a niche for yourself. You should give your own contribution on other blogs too. This will help you to make the new readers aware about yourself.

You can write on issues which will help readers to save valuable time and money. You will realize that readers love to read posts which teach them about saving time and money. Try to write on topics on which you have a high level of expertise. This will help you to give useful tips on the same to your readers who will find your posts very useful and practical.

If you can write on issues which are able to give a solution, you will get a very good response as people are always on the lookout to get a solution to their endless problems which are common nowadays. Finally you can also write posts which narrate a story in an interesting format. This too will be appreciated by your readers.

Ways to Find New RSS Subscribers for Your Blog

RSS feed (really simple syndication) is a technology that enables you to keep track of updates on your favorite blogs and websites.

1. If getting new RSS subscribers for your blog is turning to be a problem for you, try the following ten tips to find new ways to get subscribers for your blog:

2. Always reward your new RSS subscribers so that they feel happy. When you offer any free information or e-book, you will definitely be able to attract new readers for your blogs. You will also be able to retain your older subscribers too by this method.

3. One way of getting new RSS subscribers is by offering your RSS feed to email services. You will be able to tap new RSS readers in this manner with the email format.

4. Try to attract new subscribers by inserting images in your blog link. This will help you to target readers who are choosy about reading plain text blogs. Try using a RSS button on your blog and see the difference it can make in getting you new subscribers.

5. A catchy way to get RSS subscribers for your blog would be to come up with an effective campaign for your blog. This will ensure that your blog gets promoted to new readers who will then get converted into RSS subscribers in a short period of time.

6. You should also make your blogs more popular by getting your URL printed out on your business cards. This will help you to promote your blogs without using the

internet, thus ensuring a new form of audience. This will help you to get more RSS subscribers for your blogs.

7. You can make good use of different methods to get new RSS subscribers for your blogs. Every set-up on the internet has its own list of readers. You will be able to get them diverted to your blog by using a variety of methods rather than just concentrating on a single method to get new readers.

8. You also have the option of getting new RSS subscribers for your blog by being a guest on other blogs. Try to give interesting matter on such blogs. It will help you to get your blogs exposed to a larger audience of readers.

9. In order to get more RSS subscribers you need to make RSS more popular among those who have no idea about what RSS is all about. Once you have done that it will

be much easier to target the people who you have helped in knowing more about RSS.

10. Social bookmarking sites too can be used by you effectively to bring in new RSS subscribers for your blogs.

11. Finally you should use a subscription landing page which will exclusively cater to anyone who wants to subscribe to your blogs.

Now let us see how you can drive more traffic to your blog using blog marketing in the next chapter.

Chapter 4 – Criteria to be a great blogger

Write compelling copy

When Robert's blog was pulling in a lot of traffic of which most were turning into clients his friends were surprised as to how he did it. Robert told them the secret of his success. It is powerful copy of his blog and newsletters. When people read them they were curious to know what the site has in store and visited his blog. There are many online marketers who will agree with this. Powerful copy can get the reader interested in the subject and induce him/her to learn more about it. Sales letter only sells the product. If a person is not interested then he/she may simply delete the sales letter without even reading it. A powerful copy should not push anything down the throat of the reader. It should state facts in an attractive manner.

There are more than ten points to note while getting copywriting for your blog. After all you need to turn the reader into a client. Every reader is a prospective client. So your web copy should be compelling at the same time appealing to the reader.

- First and foremost be direct and succinct. Start with a clear statement of what you're offering. Also ensure that proper grammar and English is used. See to it that there is no turning of verbs into nouns. Keep the sentences short and precise. Maintaining a single voice will ensure that the reader can visualize what he is reading. Writing in a listing format makes the copy look well thought-out and lucid. Headline is responsible for most of your response. So let the headline be grabbing. It can be in question form or points. For example- Is your weight loss routine working? or 5 steps to weight loss

- Also describe the product or services you are selling. This will make the reader curious to know, more about the product and whether there is any use for him with it. Describe your product in detail and also say how different it is from your competitors. Talk to your clients as if they're in person. Make them understand that you have thought out about all the problems that are sure to arise and have taken measures to overcome them. This will show you as a genuine supplier and will make the reader believe you.

- Secondly make your copywriting search engine optimized. By placing appropriate keywords throughout the pages you can optimize the blog to get traffic through search engines. If you have popular keywords throughout your copy, search engines will include your blog in search results for those terms. Use innovative keywords that will drive additional traffic to your blog. A keyword rich content with title tag will always draw traffic to your blog.

- Once traffic is drawn how do you convert readers into buyers? Here is where you need to be more personal and direct with your prospective client. Be honest and share all information regarding your product with online readers. The more you tell the more you sell. Describe the benefits of your product, compare it with the competitive product and explain why it is better to buy your product. These will certainly help the reader appreciate the product and induce him to buy it.

- In blog marketing your copyrighting is your sales man. Keep it direct; honest, and serious and most important, avoid humor. Your copy should be convincing and precise.

- Add testimonials of your clients. Make them interesting in a story format. Add a picture to it. This will make it exciting and authentic. Story telling has helped sell many products online. People get absorbed with stories. They visualize and get attracted to it. If you have a client who is willing to share his or her fears and apprehensions before buying your product and how your product changed his life, then go for it. Add visuals as well as a video. This is sure to go well with your readers. The first line of your story should be attractive and eye catching. Only then the reader will continue reading the rest of the story.

As a story teller your aim is to ensure that your reader feels that this product will help him get rid of his problem. Convincing your reader about this will turn him into a buyer and for that you need an interesting and arresting story. For example:

'If I can make $1000 per day, so can you'.

This line is sure to grab the attention of the reader.

How to write a blog post?

While writing a blog post, make it instructional and add examples. Case studies or testimonials are a great way to make the reader believe in you. Also add graphs, images, surveys, and statistics to support your claims. Let your blog post have an attitude. Be direct and don't beat round the bush.

Maintain high standards while blogging. Never lie. Readers will come to know as there is an overload of information on the internet. Be honest, direct and trustworthy. That'll endear you to the reader.

- Format every blog post so that it's easy for people to scan.
- Most of the time readers online just scan through the pages.
- Keep the page A4 in size. Don't widen it.
- Use headings and sub headings.
- Numbering and bullet points show clarity

- Use short paragraphs. Writing long paragraphs will not interest the reader and he'll skip reading it.
- Use punctuation and bold fonts.
- Use an attractive blog theme. Give importance to background color.
- Use attractive images and videos. Let the image size be big.
- Be consistent and update regularly.

Once you keep in mind all the above mentioned tips to write a blog post you're sure to get readers. In case you have old blog posts that are relevant even now, rewrite them with an attractive heading and subheadings. Along with a new image repost it as a new post. Readers who missed it the first time may get to read it this time around.

Start a mailing list

You've a great blog and you're regularly updating it. You asked all your friends and family to visit your blog and comment on your posts. Your blog has a beautiful lay out and pleasing colors. The subject matter is also topical and relevant. So far so good. Then why aren't you getting any traffic? Why the free download isn't, (you've offered on your blog) not used? Why is it you've no organic traffic? Why, why and more whys? Well the answer to all your why's lie in promoting your blog. You need to advertise about your blog. You need to write emails with a personal touch so that you get organic traffic. To do that you need email addresses. You need to prepare a list of email addresses that'll help you to promote your blog. Email list is a very important tool to attract traffic. Just as you promote products through hoardings and pamphlets/ fliers in the physical world, you need to send emails regularly to prospective customers in the virtual world. Without a mailing list your blog is as good as dead.

It is not enough to have a great product and an attractive blog. You may be the most brilliant guy; yet if you don't promote your blog through mailing list then your efforts go in vain. There are companies like Justdial from where you can buy mailing addresses. These are collected from people at the Mall or shopping complexes. Many email lists are prepared from telecom directories as well. Utility companies sell their customers email addresses. Credit card companies also do the same. Here the question arises if all those addresses are your target audience. Well, that's a good question. Not all may be your audience. 50% of them may be your audience. As a thumb rule in any mailing list only 20% respond to your email and visit your blog. Half of them simply go away after visiting the first page. Only the other half visits your entire blog. Out of this a few may communicate with you for more information about your product.

It is not that once you send out the list you can sit back and watch. You need to constantly monitor how many people have opened your email and read it. Then correspond with them on a personal level. Don't try to sell your product.

Simply ask them for their opinion and what they're looking for. Take feedback and analyze it. That'll give you an idea of what people are looking for. Email lists are the ideal way to drive in new traffic and higher click through rates.

Keep adding to your email list from time to time. A good amount of traffic surely comes from lists. Address the pain points of your customer in a blog post and email the link to them. You can always tailor make your emails to suit your prospective clients. That'll help to get instant click through rates.

If your blog is down due to maintenance or other issues let your clients know about it through email. You can also make a video of your blog post and upload it on YouTube and send a link to the audience. This will help to retain your reader base. Email is the best way to contact a customer. It is personal and trustworthy. Give value for the effort and time your reader gives you. An ideal email list should be somewhere around one hundred thousand (100,000) email addresses. Here the bounce rate will be around 25%. Many emails will not be operational.

Don't use your personal Gmail account to send bulk emails. You'll be breaking opt-in rules of marketing. Use an email service provider. There are many out there. Before you choose one make sure that you're offered –

- To build a large database
- Send emails to multiple addresses at a time
- Methods to follow up
- Have a sign up form on your blog

Also see to it that you get help from them on how to set up an account, monitor the emails, and assess the progress and also that their customer relations is quick and helpful.

It is noted that email lists get a ten times higher conversion than social media campaigns. The reason being it's personal, targeted, one on one, and it's your own. Big businesses learned the trick a long time ago. They conduct social media campaigns and prepare an 'opt in' list on their website/ blogs and then communicate with their prospective customers through email. This is the best way to grow your email list. It is a long term investment where the returns are high. Readers get latest information at a low cost for a long period.

You can also offer incentives to your customers. That'll induce them to introduce their friends to your blog.

1. For example – you've 250 email addresses and readers who visit your blog regularly to read your posts.
2. Offer them freebies and gifts to introduce (referrals) 5 of their friends to your blog. This will automatically get you 1000+ readers.
3. Keep adding readers by sending emails constantly to these 1000 readers.
4. Be careful not to spam them. Else it doesn't take much time to click on the spam button.

5. Ask for feedback from the readers once they receive the freebie. Communicate with them to keep them engaged as well as know about your product. This will help to iron out glitches, if any.

6. Don't lie to people. Be honest and give the freebies you promised. That is what will help you in the long run.

7. The copywriting should be truthful and fulfill the promises you made to them.

8. Finally have a relationship with your list. Remember your email list is the only way you can reach your target audience online. Once you've it in place building up will not be a tough task.

Chapter 5 - Custom blog creation and SEO

Blogs are here to stay and every website should be complimented with a blog. If you don't want to utilize your business resources in maintaining a website, you should check the custom blog creation option. Even if you have a website, you can still maintain a blog separately. There are a number of reasons why you should use a blog for your online marketing needs. Don't worry if you are not very net savvy, you can maintain a blog very easily once it has been created for you. You have the freedom of posting matter on your blog everyday or as and when you get the time to post matter on it.

A blog is very easy to maintain when compared to a website. You don't need to be a master at programming or web designing. Just feed in your text matter and add a couple of photos and your blog is all set to connect you to your audience. Try to name your blog in such a way, that it has important keywords which are linked to your online business.

All the necessary tools to create a blog are available readymade online. Word Press and BlogSpot offer you colorful themes and add on's, that can be helpful to make an attractive blog. There is no need for a professional anymore. The layout, color and design and themes are all available for free.

One important reason why you need to have a customized blog for your business needs is because search engines always rate blogs very highly. The more you can update your blog, the more it improves its chances of getting popular with the search engines. A blog is a neat way to distribute content as there are no complications involved in the creation of a blog post. You can get subscribers to your blog who will be regularly informed of your latest blogs by a number of updating services. RSS feeds, social media and email marketing help you to make your updates known to the world.

Once you use keywords and optimize your blog for search engine purposes it automatically indexes your blog and notifies you. Your blog starts to appear on organic searches like first page on Google. For example – if your blog is about yoga, then whenever someone is searching for information about yoga, they may get to see your blog on the search results. This depends upon various factors like SEO, regular updates, having long tail keywords, short keywords, joining the Adwords program, etc. Till now all these are free tools available online.

If you don't like the readymade themes available online, you can always hire a web designer to design a special blog theme for you. The web designer may buy a specific theme and work on it to suit to your needs. Or the designer can simply create a new theme for your blog. This depends upon your budget. Once the blog is created, update it regularly. Keep in mind about SEO and keyword popularity before you start writing a blog post. Sprinkle keywords throughout the post without going overboard. Let it look natural.

Whenever you submit a post on your blog, it gets indexed within a day by Google. I love blogs because they allow me to get regular feedback from my target audience. I can then get back to the people who have given me the feedback and improvise on what has been suggested by them. Now that you know about all the tricks connected with custom blog creation, go ahead and make it work for your online business needs.

SEO (search engine optimization)

These three words have changed the dynamics of the 21st century. Search engine optimization is a process through which you get natural/ organic traffic to your blog/ website. There are three major search engines and they are Google, Yahoo, and Bing. Of the three Google is the most popular one. When users enter queries into the search engine (using keywords or phrases) the search engine examines its index and provides a listing (the search results) of all the websites/ blogs that as per its algorithmic logic, are the most relevant (best matching) to the search terms. The website/ blogs listing is usually provided ten to a page (Google follows this), with a short summary containing the document's title and sometimes a small part of the text.

SEO techniques belong to two main categories of that which search engines agree and disagree. These techniques are respectively termed as 'White Hat' and 'Black Hat'. While most SEO practitioners utilize time tested ethical methods for search engine optimization, there are many black sheep who resort to unethical means (methods which search engine administrators disapprove of as being unfair which are termed as 'Black Hat' tactics.

An SEO technique is considered to be 'white hat' if it confirms to search engine's guidelines; does not involve any deception; and ensures that the search engine indexed content is the content the reader will get to see on the website/ blog. On the other hand, 'black hat' SEO tactics try to improve rankings by trying to fool the search engine algorithm by such methods as 'keyword stuffing' (packing in excessive numbers of keywords), 'spamdexing', using hidden text which will be seen by the spider but not by the user etc.

Websites/ blogs using black hat tactics may be penalized by the web crawler or through manual review. Keywords are search terms (words or phrases) that people are using to locate whatever it is that they are searching for on the net. Keywords are, in fact, the 'wonder words' that prompt Search Engines to list your website on the search results page (through a keywords matching process) when people (likely potential customers) search for those terms. A proper selection of keywords is therefore critical in ensuring that 'hits' on your website are maximized. Try to think what keywords your customers are likely to use for searching your product category (competitors' websites can be a useful source!). Many online Keyword Research Tools are also available.

A keyword can actually be one or more words and you can choose more than one keyword for your product. Sometimes a set of keywords which are searched for exactly as keyed-in or keywords within " " or [ ] form a keyword phrase. People search the net in different ways for the product or information category they are looking for; some in broad terms and others in a very specific manner. You should, therefore, have a judicious mix of four types (*Broad match, Phrase match, Exact match* and *Negative match*) keywords to increase the chances of your website receiving hits from various types of searches undertaken by potential clients.

When we talk of keywords, we may be referring to the use of keywords in the Text or to those used in the metatags (the little lines of text that are placed between the <head> tag and the </head> tag) in the HTML code of your website; the metatags are designed to give search engines instructions on what your page is all about and how they should process information related to it.

The right keywords are the very foundations of your entire online marketing campaign. You must ensure that your website has plenty of relevant keywords and metatags to attract search engines.

Metatags

As explained, metatags are text written into the HTML code that describes your website to the search engines. They influence the way in which your site appears in the search results and often cause an increase of traffic to your site. Metatags are not visible in the browser window to people visiting your site (unless they view your website's HTML by selecting 'view source'). While there are several metatags that can be used, the most useful are the *Keywords* tag and the *Description* tag.

Keywords metatag

The use of the right keywords is crucial – but the question is, how do you find them? The first practical step is to try and think as customers searching for your product category would do. This will throw up a number of leads (keywords) which you can work upon and expand. Competitors' websites can also be a very useful source. You can also take the help of numerous online Keyword Research Tools that are available. Once you have finalized and ranked (in order of importance) your keywords, you need to insert them in the metatag of your website HTML code.

The keywords tag should contain your most important (relevant) keywords and phrases (ideally not more than 10 words). These words can be separated by commas, spaces or both and you should try to avoid repeating any of the words more than, say, three times. An example of a Keywords metatag may be as follows:

<meta name = "keywords" content = "keyword 1, Keyword 2, Keyword 3"/>

Page titles (title tag)

The page title or the <Title> tag is the text in the title bar (or windows bar) of the browser window seen by a visitor. It gives people an insight into what your website is about and is also used by search engines and some directories for indexing and listing the link to your website. The Title tag is, therefore, one of the most important elements of your webpage and you absolutely *must* include the most important keyword phrase(s) in it. A correct Page Title will increase your website ranking and encourage 'click throughs'.

There is a limit to how long the title text can be (for example, Google allows 66 characters including spaces and punctuations) and you need to be very careful to ensure that the title phrase that you write makes sense. It is advisable to develop a page title that you can use for search engine submission, directory linkages as well as for links to your website. The title tag should, typically, include the website name, the location if applicable and keywords that may get attention. A title tag may look as follows:

<title>XYZ Company, Victoria, Australia – Car Parts, Automotive spares</title>

Description metatag

Correctness of descriptions and relevancy of page titles together encourage 'click throughs' (hits) and increase the chances of quality leads. Normally a couple of lines long, description metatags provide a string of textual information relating to your website.

The description, like the title, is of critical importance because it is an expansion of the truncated information appearing in the title, enabling Search engines, Directories (and Links) to utilize the information related to your site. You should ensure that the description contains enough relevant information (by including keywords) to lure traffic to your site. Including keywords also helps to increase your keyword rankings. The description metatag is similar to the Keyword metatag, as shown in the following example:

<meta name="description" content="ABC Coy. sells Car Parts, Automotive spares/>

Keywords in text

Keywords and their use in text or body of your web page and their importance from the perspective of Search Engines has already been discussed under Section 4. Keywords and keyword phrases in your text (content) and their variations, enable your website to respond (be selected) to a wide range of search terms (broad; specific; exact etc) that may be used by potential customers. They help to draw in more traffic and also to assure users that they are at the right location. The *Keyword Density* (ratio of keywords to the total words in a page) should optimally be between 2 and 5%.

Keywords in links

Once your site is operational, apart from links to the sub-pages of your website, you need to build links to other websites to increase traffic and to improve your rankings. For best results (increased 'hits') and higher 'points' from search engines on the parameter of links to your website, the links should be embedded in specific keywords or phrases (and not on your domain name or name of your company etc). In fact, one of the major factors influencing your search engine ranking is the keywords used in links to your page. The keyword or phrase should be included in the anchor text of every link, as for example:

<A href = "URL"> keyword phrase</a>

Keywords in images

Most web pages today need to include text and images. An image is displayed when the HTML code for the image gives directions to the server on the location of the image, for retrieval. However Search Engines can read only text. Hence images given an 'alt image' tag, containing a keyword or keyword phrase as shown in the example below, can match the description with the content of the site for easy retrieval of the image. This improves click throughs and rankings.

<img src = "URL" alt = "keyword or phrase">

Get indexed in Google with blogs

Getting indexed in Google with blogs is no different than getting a web-site indexed. Of course for a novice it is always advisable to go with the tried and tested. First time bloggers never had it so easy. Did you know that blogger.com and Google search engine are both owned by Google?

Why bother to know? Because, if you are blogging from blogger.com your blog gets automatically indexed in Google search engine. And clearly that is a huge step forward. One can avoid all kinds of snags while getting indexed with the largest and most popular search engine. But in case you prefer to blog from a different provider or you simply want to use your own web-site for blogging. What happens then? First of all you should submit your URL to Google. It is quite simple really.

Go to the page:

http://www.google.com/addurl/?continue=/add url and follow the instructions. In a week's time your site will start showing on Google search. But that may not be enough. A nifty piece of work would be to add a word on your blog and link it to one of the posts on the Google blog or in any article on TechCrunch. This will make your blog visible and appealing to the spiders crawling around the net. Whenever they visit the above blogs, which they will often, they will acknowledge your blog.

To get the attention of the indexing services or search engines a few strategic comments on similar blogs will be useful. This will establish your legitimacy in the blogosphere. There are many forums and communities where you can declare your presence. Search for these and hitch your blog to them.

There is no substitute to good content. I will repeat this till you drop dead with boredom.

Chapter 6 - Blog Marketing

Increase your traffic

The World Wide Web is, well, worldwide. And the din and noise is almost overwhelming. As a blogger how do you make yourself be heard? How do you market your blog and thoughts?

The first thing you require in this rat race is patience. Remember the story of the hare and the tortoise? Slow and steady wins the race. First and foremost create a niche for yourself. Your blog should reflect your passion for the subject you write on. There is no point in half hearted attempts. There are so many unfulfilled blogs out there in the blogosphere, it makes you weep. Once you have chosen your subject/ niche, write, write and write. Create content at a steady pace. Daily entries on your blog won't hurt. The next step is to be seen and heard.

For a lay blogger blogger.com is ideal. BlogSpot and WordPress are also good. Everything happens almost automatically and tools are available which make blogging a pleasurable experience rather than a maze of technology. Your site is automatically indexed by Google which can be a great beginning.

Choose an apt name

Choose a blog address that describes your blog best. For example if you're writing about mobile technology your blog name should be like www.allaboutmobiles.com . This explains for itself. If you're having a blog on gardening then it can be www.greenthumb.com. This clearly denotes what your blog is all about. Once you've decided on the name start filling your blog with content. Upload colorful images, videos besides posts to make your blog look attractive. When a visitor visits your blog he/ she should be impressed with the first page. Update your blog regularly. It should have latest posts on the first page.

Social media marketing

The internet may have changed your lives forever, but the social media movement has taken you to another plane altogether. It cannot simply be called a revolution. Social networking has been a game changer which has brought about cataclysmic changes and upheavals in the way we work and play. As things stand today, social media sites have become highly specialized, catering to a variety of needs. Facebook, Instagram, Tumblr, Pinterest, MySpace, Snapchat, are all huge social platforms used extensively all around the world.

All of us are on social media. There are forums where you can join and post comments. Give judicious comments and add threads where others are likely to see. This is a good way to attract viewership. Several social sites have communities which you may find useful to participate in.

As it generally happens with any new technology or system, there are few dark clouds in the social networking horizon. According to a Nielson report, organizations are losing a staggering amount of man hours because their employees often engage in chatting up with friends through social media sites. Some even equate it to a mass hysteria happening on the cyberspace. The benefits of course far outweigh the disadvantages. Companies are finding new ways to leverage the power of social media and have come up with highly innovative ideas to empower themselves and their employees.

There are numerous social media sites catering to zillions of applications. The primary challenge for online marketers is to sift through the white noise of social chatter and create marketing opportunities. The value proposition though evident has to be extracted like we dig out gold ore from the mines. Marketing experts have identified forums on social sites as the main interface for attracting customer. The selection and development of forums on social sites is not only an art but a science. The quest for eyeballs has become extremely competitive and social media gurus are using increasingly sophisticated tools to discover and retain loyal customers.

Quora.com is one such forum where you can find all kinds of people.

Facebook

The king of social sites is obviously Facebook. The membership of the site has been reported to be over one billion which is truly humungous. No doubt marketers are salivating at the prospect of reaching out to this captive consumer base. Assuming that only a fraction of this crowd is active on Facebook, it still makes for a huge amount. A new trend which has been noticed is the evolution of geographically localized social sites. Facebook has a massive following all around the world. Facebook has followers from 180 countries and is a world of its own.

Not only are social sites spatially dispersed but are also catering to niche markets. LinkedIn is a specialized site catering to professionals looking for a job and business opportunities. Social bookmarking sites have taken off in a big way. Digg, Reddit, Stumbleupon and Delicious are some notable bookmarking sites.

How will social media look like in future? Experts, as usual, have different views, but one thing is for sure – social media is here to stay. Probably we will see a coalescing of major media sites into much bigger entities. At the same time niche sites catering to small but specialized groups, differentiated by professions, religion, region and taste, will emerge. These sites would typically have a few hundred to a thousand users.

The power of social media can only be harnessed by joining the movement than looking at it from the sidelines. A creative plunge into the social waters is the best way to learn and swim in it. Social media is a movement which definitely influences opinions and decision making. The enormous opportunities offered by it must be tapped and harnessed. In fact, some online marketers have even called it the easiest path to success. When you consider the fact that marketing on social media costs almost nothing, the entire concept looks like a steal. Meanwhile the millions who are using this medium for fun and pleasure will go on with their merrymaking without any letup.

Twitter

Twitter has taken on an iconic dimension and is probably the most used application on earth. This social media platform allows only 140 characters yet it is so powerful that a single tweet can bring down a government. By building up an audience, your one tweet will enable your blog post to go viral. As soon as you update your blog, tweet the link and see the traffic trooping to your blog. This is an amazing way to increase traffic. Look for customers who show interest to your product on Twitter. Give them an 'opt in' on your blog. That is a way to collect email addresses. For example – if you're selling running shoes, follow runners like Usain Bolt and his followers on Twitter. If you follow a thousand people, five hundred will follow you back. Now entice these followers to visit your blog. This is the best way to increase traffic to your blog.

Google +

There are around 2.2 billion users on Google + and the number is growing. Soon Google will make it mandatory for all Gmail users to have a Google + profile. It has been noted that 440 million are active users every month. You've a readymade audience for your blog right here. On Google +, the link to your blog post is visible both to your audience as well as organic readers. Google even index your blog post that in turn appears on search results. Make your Google + account SEO optimized. Include keywords and relevant links on your 'About Page'. Link back to your blog. Google allows you to use bullet points on your 'About Us Page'.

Google Hangout is an amazing place to get all your prospective customers together. Webinars, work functions can be ideal platforms to talk to your audience. Google Events have custom made invites that can be used for promoting events. This will help to increase awareness about your blog. Engage with influencers and actively grow your community.

LinkedIn

LinkedIn is a business, employment oriented social networking site that boasts of 467 million users. Out of this 100 million accounts are active. This social media was started 15 years ago and now become a hot bed for professionals and freelancers alike. Anybody from the age of 18 and above has a LinkedIn profile. Search for people in your niche and send invites to them. Once they reach your LinkedIn profile, have arresting content and a link to your blog. That'll help you to increase footfalls to your blog. You can create 'connections' in this manner and turn them into customers.

Online PR

The widespread use of Internet is bringing many changes in the way business is conducted. Entrepreneurs are taking their businesses online and generating enormous profits through advertising. There has been a major shift in the online arena. This has led to the birth of online advertising.

What is online advertising?

Advertising has finally transcended the traditional areas of print, television, and radio and is making its presence felt in the online arena. This has spawned a whole new industry, which concentrates on marketing products, services, and organizations in the area of the Internet. E-commerce is one of the most common models of online advertising. Online advertising has helped many businesses show case their product to the global market without restricting to one single area. With Geo positioning advertisements the same site can have local advertisements from different countries simultaneously from where they are viewed. This has helped websites earn good revenue. With a single website they are able to generate income across continents. A popular greetings site makes a minimum of one million dollars per month thanks to geo positioning of advertisements on their website.

The scope for online advertising has developed a great deal. There are a number of methods that are commonly used by entrepreneurs and companies who are seeking to improve their online presence. These methods include email marketing, blog marketing, search engine marketing and affiliate marketing. But this is only the tip of the iceberg. There are a number of other methods that are used by businesses that aspire to reach out to a greater online consumer base.

The rise of online advertising has given the small player opportunity to make his presence felt in the international arena. Take the example of a medium-sized loan provider who does not have the financial ability to promote his services through commercials or billboard advertisements. In the real world, this means that a small loan provider can only rely on word of mouth and goodwill of people that they have serviced. Clearly, in the long run this cannot account for much. But when the same loan provider takes his work on to level playing field of internet, he suddenly has access to an entire new market.

The great thing about online advertising is that one can directly access the target customer. This could be through emails to the specific customer or through leads on sites that this customer frequents. Such methods are also cheaper in the long run because one does not have to invest in a large sales force. Moreover, exorbitant rates for billboard advertisements and television commercials are eliminated in the case of online advertising.

Pay per click is another method through which businesses earn revenue in online advertising. When a person clicks on the advertisement that is positioned on a relevant website, he is the right target audience, since he is interested to know more about the ad. This ensures that only your target audience gets to see your online advertisement. For every ten clicks you can be assured of a sale. Isn't that good enough?

Online video directories for products are a great initiative of interactive advertising. The directories and television advertising, balance with each other allowing the viewer to watch advertisements of a variety of products. If the customer is interested, he communicates immediately through Email or phone. The response to online advertising is very high and conversion rates are also high. Telebrands was one of the largest television advertising brands from 1996 to 2003.

Businesses today have to tap the online markets. Online advertising is a medium which reaches out to the entire world. No doubt, businesses and individuals are turning to the internet to realize their goals.

Other ways to promote your blog

It's very important to promote your blog in the right manner after you have written it completely. The right amount of promotion will help you to target your potential readers. Here are ten different ways to promote your next blog post:

1. You can promote your blog by providing its link in your newsletter which you normally send to a list of people maintained by you. Use this way to promote your blog only when you have written your best blog posts.
2. Another interesting way to promote your blog post is to write a follow up post to your previous blog. There should be some linkage to the previous blog in your latest blog. This will provide you with much

needed impetus to promote your previous blog.

3. You can take the help of other bloggers to promote your new blog posts. Remember you will not get help from every blogger you know. Stick to the bloggers who are ready to help you out in making readers aware about your blog post. Only approach those bloggers whose blogs will have some connection with your blog post.

4. You should promote your new blog posts by linking them in your email signatures. This too will help you in getting traffic towards your blog posts.

5. You can make good use of social messaging sites to promote your blog post. This will help you to divert traffic to your blog post.

6. You can also promote your blog posts by advertising them. This should be done by you only if you have kept aside a small budget for your blog's advertising. Do

advertising for only those blog posts which are special in quality and content.

7. You can become a guest blogger on another blogger's blog. It will help you to tap new audience for the type of blog posts which are written by you.

8. Social bookmarking is another handy way to promote your next blog post. You can choose the best bookmarking sites for promoting your blog posts.

9. You can also promote your next blog post by linking your new blog anywhere within the contents of your previous blogs.

10. Finally, you can also leave your blog posts links at blogs written by other bloggers. This should only be done by you if your blog is strongly related to the topic which has been covered up by the blogger who has written the blog.

Chapter 7 – Internet marketing & blogging

Ten years ago when JC Penny reported a five million dollar profit through internet marketing, during their holiday sales, the world sat up and watched in wonder. This led to the birth of Internet marketing. The widespread use of the internet is bringing in new changes in the way business is conducted. Entrepreneurs are taking their businesses online and enormous profits are being generated. There has been a major shift to the online arena. This has spawned a whole new industry, which concentrates on marketing products, services, and organizations in the area of the Internet. E-commerce is one of the most common models of internet marketing. One of the first sites to get into internet marketing with a vengeance was Amazon. Everyone else just followed suit. Some sites have links that lead to other sites; yet another model for the internet marketing world.

These days, internet marketing has developed to a great deal. There are a number of methods that are commonly used by entrepreneurs and companies who are seeking to improve the online presence of their businesses. These methods include email marketing, blog marketing, search engine marketing and affiliate marketing. But this is only the tip of the iceberg which is internet marketing. There are a number of other methods that are used by businesses that aspire to reach out to a greater online consumer base.

For instance, search engine optimization is a major affair as far as internet marketing is concerned. With search engines bringing in the most revenues, businesses are keen to crack the code that brings sites to the main index of major search engines like Google and Yahoo.

Internet marketing has given the small player also an opportunity to make his presence felt in the international arena. Take the example of a medium-sized loan provider that does not have the financial ability to promote his services through commercials or billboard advertisements. In the real world, this means that the small loan provider can only rely on word of mouth and the goodwill of the people that he has serviced. Clearly, this cannot account for much in the long run. But when the same loan provider takes its work on to the level playing field of the internet, it suddenly has access to an entire new market.

The loan provider builds a website to advertise his business and products and also has a blog to go with it. He constantly updates the blog and offers a link to one of his website pages. These pages are search engine optimized and so get indexed by Google. This attracts traffic.

The great thing about internet marketing is that you can directly access the target customer. This could be through emails to the specific customer or through leads on sites that the customer frequents. Such methods also fall cheaper in the long run because one does not have to invest in a large sales force. Moreover, the exorbitant rates for billboard advertisements and television commercials are greatly reduced in the case of internet marketing.

Internet marketing comprises of Email marketing, social media marketing through Google +, Facebook, Instagram, Twitter, Snapchat and Flickr. Video marketing through YouTube, blog marketing, affiliate marketing, and viral marketing are all means of internet marketing services. Having your own website acts like a virtual office as well as advertisement to your business. SEO and Google analytics are also strategies that can help with your internet marketing endeavors. Optimize your web pages/ blogs and see the traffic trooping into your blog. You'll be amazed by this greatest phenomenon of the 21st century. Try internet marketing services on your blog and hear the jingle of money in your account.

Email marketing for your blog

There was a time when Email was another tool to stay in touch with friends and relatives around the world. Not anymore. Hotmail revolutionized Email and today Email has taken a different role altogether. It is the most favorite marketing tool for businesses all around the world. Businesses are going all out to promote their products and services to a global market. After all sitting in the U.S. you can sell your products free of cost to potential customers in Asia and Europe. Since email address is free anybody and everybody has one and you have a good database of potential customers addresses with you. Your newsletters can be emailed to them and you can see the response to gauge the result of Email marketing.

Bulk email marketing has not worked successfully because people simply delete them thinking they are junk Emails. However, opt-in lists and newsletters offer good scope for organizations seeking to promote their business.

This is because potential customers choose to get these emails because they are interested in what a company has to offer. Carefully see to it that you build up a genuine customer base and that you are able to keep them as your regular clients.

Building that relationship with your subscriber may not be easy, but it is not rocket science. Here are a few tips that you could follow when starting your email marketing campaign:

- Create a subject line that holds the attention of your subscriber.

- Offer valuable new information in every email. Do not just dish out the same old jargon. Provide tips and tricks that will keep your subscriber thirsting for more.

- Convey more in less words.

- Remember that this is a business letter. Personalize it but maintain a degree of formality. Remember that you are not on back-slapping terms with your subscribers.

- Encourage feedback.

- Avoid negative responses in your Email messages. Practice effective and skillful communication.

- Make your Email messages mobile friendly. Nowadays everyone has a smart phone and is checking Emails on phone.

- Have attractive and eye catching images relating to your business. Link it to your blog.

- Create your campaign and see how effective it is.

- Measure your success and iron out the glitches.

There are several other aspects that could ensure that your email marketing campaign yields results. Find out what works for you.

Vlog (video log)

A blog could describe the product in detail as well as show some pictures. But a Vlog holds video of the product and you can explain in detail to your customers about your business.

What is a Vlog?

Vlog is the short form for video log. You can not only read about the business or person but also see them on video. This is the future of blog. Some say that this will be the ideal way to market your product. It's personalized and people can watch what they want to and not what is available. This is the best marketing tool for businesses, freelancers and product manufacturers.

Another use of Vlog can be for dating and matrimonial purposes. Instead of paying to be on one of the sites that charge exorbitant rates, Vlog will be ideal for dating and matrimonial alliances. You can not only speak to the person but also see him/her to make your decision. Not only can you see an individual, you will come to know about his life if he has been Vlogging for a while.

If a person can be innovative, Vlog can be used to post your resume on the internet. Instead of writing about yourself and your expertise and area of operation, shoot your own video and present it on your blog site for people to see. The impact this will create is certainly worth the trouble.

The first Vlogs, began appearing on the internet in late 2003, early 2004. Steve Garfield was the first one to launch his video blog on January 1, 2004. As technology improves with time Vlogs are here to stay and improve in speed and picture quality as web 2.0 tools also are getting enhanced. When Mr. Garfield first spoke to the world through his computer, a new world opened up for internet users and blogging took a new shape in the name of video log i.e. Vlog.

Skype is good as a Vlog for businesses. You Tube is the best Vlog site to promote your blog.

YouTube/Video marketing

It all started with Justin Beiber who at the age of thirteen uploaded his music video on YouTube and received a million hits in no time. He became a singing sensation overnight and music record companies vied to sign him for big amounts. That is how everyone started jumping on to this bandwagon. People started uploading their videos on YouTube to get noticed by the world. Singers, dancers, actors and film promotions started happening on YouTube. Film trailers were launched here and gauging the response it could be decided whether the film will be a hit or not. YouTube became an important marketing tool for individuals and companies alike. It took a different dimension all together and nowadays anything and everything is uploaded on YouTube.

Study tutorials to teach kids school education, make up tutorials to teach people how to apply makeup, cookery (this is big business) are all uploaded on YouTube. These videos receive excellent viewership and based on it the businesses pay people to advertise their products. There are reviewers who even make videos talking about garments and other consumer products.

If your business is in technology then you can showcase your products and talk about them. Car manufacturers display their latest model cars on YouTube. Practically anything and everything is promoted through YouTube. It is very easy and simple to use YouTube. The platform is user friendly. All you need is a Gmail address or Facebook log in. Use it to upload your products. You can also share these videos on your Facebook page and blog. It helps both ways.

Growing plants, agriculture, landscaping gardens, promoting real estate are all done on YouTube. If your blog is about fitness and weight loss then you can promote fitness equipment, diets and weight loss supplements. You can also upload videos of healthy salads, protein shakes and other fitness foods to attract viewers. Link all these to your blog.

Visually your videos need to be appealing and have soothing voiceovers. You come to know the number of people who have viewed your video and also how many have liked them. Viewers can also share, republish, find the way to your blog and subscribe to your channel. The beauty here is all this can be done free of cost.

The best way to promote your product is to watch your competitor's videos and see which videos have received the highest number of views. That'll give you an idea of what viewers wish to see and you can tailor make your videos accordingly.

Conduct webinars and interview with the CEO of the company. These will add a personal touch to your product.

Get experts to review your products for a fee. This will instantly increase traffic. If the reviewer has a blog request him to share the video. That'll get you more footfalls to your blog. Testimonials of users can help to increase traffic. Make videos of their experience with your product and upload them.

The most important aspect of promoting your product is through volume. Have as many videos as possible and upload them on YouTube. At the same time give a link to the editorial calendar on your blog. This will help to increase traffic to your blog. Do these for a period of six months, before you have a look at the data. There should be a significant boost to your sales thanks to your blog and YouTube marketing.

You can make changes midway to your YouTube promotion, just in case it is not working as you wished. Make changes as you go along. Since it is free to upload videos on YouTube, you can promote your products free of cost. You can also talk about your blog and pull people to visit it. That'll increase traffic to your blog.

Whether you're selling a product or offering services anything can be promoted on YouTube.

Chapter 8 - How to use your blog for profit

Darren Rowse, an Australian was a regular church goer. He was working at a departmental store till the year 2002. He started blogging as a hobby about church and religious issues. He blogged about living in Australia, the Michael Jackson case, and issues he found interesting. He also blogged on various platforms and wrote on several issues. His innovative and thought provoking posts attracted many visitors and his blogs became popular among online readers. Those were the days when only a few people read online, unlike today. What started as a hobby became a full time occupation when he got more than ten thousand hits per day to his blog. That is how problogger.com became the most visited blog and highest revenue generating blog online in the year 2006.

Darren didn't stop there. He wrote ebooks and sold them through Clickbank.com. He also sold them through his blog. Since his blog was SEO optimized he received organic traffic from Google. He started another blog on photography (again his hobby) and uploaded beautiful pictures that people could buy for a fee. He clearly explained in his blog as to how he earns his income. He earned a handsome amount ($20,000/ per month from 2 blogs) through advertisements and guest posts. He co-founded a company b5media along with fellow bloggers Jeremy Wright, Shai Coggins and Duncan Riley. This network claims to have more than 300 blogs with a one million page views per day. It was started in his garage in the year 2006.

By the year 2007 Darren Rowse became a giant blogger online. Many television channels and print media carried his rags to riches story and that encouraged more people to blog online.

Problogger.com, digital photography school and Twitip are the three popular blogs found by

Darren Rowse. He has won many awards for his innovative income generating ideas and he has even got a mention in Forbes list. His book on 'Problogger secrets to earn a six figure income' is the fastest and highest selling book on Amazon and his net worth jumped and doubled by 2011. Today Darren Rowse is worth around 6.5 billion dollars.

What started as a hobby became a huge business and money spinner for Darren. The most important point here is, he opened a new world to fellow bloggers and showed a way to the world to make money through blogging.

Darren's story is inspiring and gives everyone a hope to achieve success in life. Imagine a department store guy becoming a successful and famous blogger? This clearly shows that anything is possible. It's just that you need enthusiasm and keenness to pursue what you feel is right.

It took Darren Rowse four years to get noticed. He continued blogging for four years without giving up. You too need to keep at it for a few years before you start seeing profits.

Make money with your blog

Blogs are not only a source of pleasure and entertainment but also for profit. Internet as a source of advertisement, marketing and sales is unparalleled. It has brought the seller and buyer closer and directly in contact. The layers of middlemen have been bypassed. The seller has gained and can offer better prices and the buyer has the opportunity to purchase products and services of his choice and at lower cost. It is a win-win situation for everyone.

Blogging has added a new dimension to business. People can now not only air their personal views on the net but also use the medium to sell their products and also of others. A cluster of new words have joined the lexicon. Affiliate marketing, Google ad sense, reciprocal links and viral marketing are the new buzzwords. For a layman, it seems a bit confusing at the beginning but mostly everyone gets a hang of it eventually. For those who get lost in the jargon there is always the unalloyed pleasure of blogging.

For the uninitiated, it is always advisable to join a free blogging service provided by well known internet companies. Google, Yahoo and Microsoft offer free blog sites. The advantage of this is obvious. Setting up your blog is easy and one can initiate an earning process almost instantly. Google Adsense is very easy to set up on blogger site. It offers both pay per click and per thousand impressions.

Affiliate marketing, where you become a member of a site which promotes other products is the next step. For example, Amazon has a good affiliate program which gives a commission of 10 % on all sales. You can sell music, books and a whole lot of other stuff as an affiliate of Amazon.

Once you become an affiliate, small program or widget (a term used on blog sites) may be required to be copied and pasted on your blog.

Again, a site like Blogger has an interface where you can easily add these widgets to your blog.

Your blog is setup for Adsense as well as an affiliate for Amazon. Now everything depends on the traffic you can generate to your blog. Always remember that content is king. Only if you have interesting things to say on your blog, people will visit. So make your site interesting and start to earn.

Drs Foster & Smith, Petco

Here's another true story of veterinary doctors Foster and Smith from Wisconsin. They own a pet blog dfs-pet-blog.com that was started in the year 1997. They regularly posted articles and blog posts on pet care and how to bring up a pet, what are the upheavals you may have to face to bring up a pet, etc. what started as an information sharing blog turned into a money spinner when they offered pet food and stuff on their blog. They also started selling pets on their blog. They sold dogs, cats, fishes, horses, reptiles and shared information on how to train them;

ponds with frogs and other aquatic animals and so on. Relentlessly they kept at it and today they earn an eye popping amount from their blog. They've more than ten authors who write about their experiences with pets. Some of them are pet trainers and so they share their experiences for a fee. They help you with all issues related to pets. Their books on pet training are available on Amazon as well as on their blog.

They are also available on social media like Facebook, Twitter and YouTube. You can watch the videos to learn about pets. In case you wish to communicate with them, you can write to them or simply post a comment on one of their blog posts. You'll be offered free advice as you're a new comer. They're into pet pharmacy, pet education and also offer boarding for pets. Their retail company is named Petco and they offer pet supplies in the USA. They're the second largest pet suppliers in America with a net worth of $1.7 billion.

Their pet blog earns around $30,000 through sale of pets and supplies, in a month. There are more than 1000,000 hits per day and they've more than 40 million mailing addresses. This clearly shows that Petco has expanded beyond Wisconsin thanks to blog marketing. There is a fundamental difference between having a blog and a website. While website is static, blog is interactive. It is always advisable to have a blog along with your website. Where as a blog can standalone without a website. That doesn't matter. So you see the importance of blogs?

You may ask these are big names and extraordinary people; do ordinary bloggers earn by blogging? Well, the answer is YES. They do earn through PPC (pay per click), guest posting, banner ads and affiliate marketing. If you've a blog and regularly post, in two to three years time you can see returns. Google pays you and it is very easy to have a payment gateway from where you can receive money into your bank account. PayPal is one of the best services available online. In your hurry to become rich don't kill the hen. Let it give one egg at a time. Be patient. That is the only secret to making money through blogging.

Whether your blog is about travel or fitness or meditation, anybody and everybody has an audience online. Remember, your blog is visible to the world and the entire world is your audience. When Paula was given the pink slip she decided to design swimsuits and sell to her friends. Designing was her passion and she was good at it since high school days. She realized that hiring a shop and keeping inventory and help, will cost her money. Her friend suggested that she go online and start a website. That too cost money; to hire a web designer, pay for internet space, etc. Instead Paula decided to start a WordPress blog for free. The tools were easily available online and Paula matched the colors and gave an attractive look to her blog. The sea and sand along with women sun bathing in gorgeous swim wears was pleasant for the eye.

Her theme was blue, green and it had a soothing effect. She wrote about her passion for designing and how she started this blog and why people should buy from her. She marketed her blog on Facebook and other social media accounts for free. She joined forums online to advertise her blog.

To start with, her friends ordered through her blog and made payments online. That encouraged Paula to get a payment gateway. She enhanced her blog and turned to email marketing. Her attractive newsletters brought footfalls to her blog. She offered freebies like a free cap with a swim wear. She had software that allowed people to try out swim wears before buying them virtually. That gave an idea to buyers as to how they would look in the outfits. She also tied up with a courier service for shipping. Paula, search engine optimized her blog and placed Meta tags and Google analytics. This helped her to keep track of her blog's performance. Slowly her blog picked up momentum and in a year's time, Paula was busy servicing orders. She hired a marketing expert to expand her business. Paula moved out of her basement and hired an office. She employed a few tailors to make the swim wears. She started to export and in a few years time Paula's brand became a big name in the swim wear business. She participated in fashion shows and her swim wear was a big hit.

Blogging is like any other business. It can help you to earn a six figure income provided you use the right tools and have loads of patience. There are many professionals who turn to blogging and use it for job opportunities. Writer John Woods maintained a blog for five years and penned his thoughts about SEO, Google analytics and other technical advancements happening in the online world. His viewers were impressed with his writing and knowledge of SEO. This helped him to land a $100,000 job with a company dealing in SEO for online marketers. John continues to blog and earn from banner ads, PPC, affiliate marketing and also his job. John used his blog as his resume.

Five years ago, Rohan was good at playing online games and decided to have his own blog about gaming software's. He wrote about how online gaming is at its nascent stage and how it can be catapulted to becoming a huge business. Since he didn't have money or the resources, he shared his ideas on his blog. His readers trooped in from the gaming sites (where he played) as well as social media. One of the readers got intrigued with Rohan's ideas and invited him to set up an online Dota championship. The prize money was big (in millions) and so was the game. Rohan advertised on his blog about the championship and offered discounts to people who joined the championship through his blog. People participated from all around the world and it became a super hit affair. Rohan got more than a million hits per day and his blog became a buzzing place for online gamers.

The secret here is to be innovative. Everything is out there for you to succeed. Keep your ears and eyes open to find opportunities. The Universe has a lot to offer you. Have faith in yourself as well as the world around you. Be focused and keep at it till you achieve success. The universal forces come together and form a potent atmosphere, pushing you to great victory.

Chapter 8 - Link Building and Blog Analytics

What do you do to sell or market your product in a world of brick and mortar? You advertise. You approach the media; newspapers, magazines, television spots and word of mouth. The internet is no different. To be heard, you have to be present at the places where your clients are. Search out other blogs on the internet who sell similar products or services. Create links to them through your blog. Those blogs which have a higher ranking in search engines should be targeted. They would be indexed much more frequently and you would also be indexed alongside.

Reciprocal links used to be quite popular. But it is rumored that the Google search engine blacklists blogs and sites which are identical. Be careful and avoid questionable sites. You are likely to be spammed by unwanted messages and a deluge of pornographic material. Beware and clean your blog from time to time of all the junk.

Submit your blog to blog directories. These contain a list of blogs and are categorized under different groups. People looking for information are likely to find you through these directories.

Having links to your blogs will help you to climb up the search ladder. Link building is an important aspect of website search engine optimization (SEO) since not all visitors to the site arrive through organic searches; many arrive from other sites or from paid ads through links. Internal links connecting different pages of the site improve navigation for visitors and web spiders. External links from **other websites not only bring additional traffic, many search engines will give higher ranking to a site based on the number of its incoming links ('link popularity').**

Considering the advantages, link building to other sites should be actively pursued once a website is operational (internal linking should be addressed at the website design stage itself). Link building

normally takes the form of 'Link Campaigns' to persuade other website owners or site managers to link to the site by providing correct information about the site and its contents. This can usually be best achieved by embedding the links in specific keywords or phrases i.e. including the right keywords in the anchor texts of the links. This also increases quality traffic and improves conversions.

Many websites include a 'Link-To-Us' function; an HTML link-to-us coding which can be copied and pasted in the webpage source code of the site wanting to link in. The essential point to remember for effective link building, however, is that other websites will consider linking to the site only if they feel that it is worth their while. Hence, firstly, the website content has to be informative and useful and secondly, the linking process should be simple; one that needs the least amount of work for linking to the site.

There was a time when you could get links just by commenting on other blogs. Google has now phased that out. Even links from article directories carry no relevance. You need to have genuine links from sites and blogs that are relevant to your niche. It is not that your blog is about yoga and you get a link from a popular pet blog. Yoga and pet as subject matters have no connection. See to it that you get links from sites that are equally serious about their niche just as you are.

Google Analytics

Many bloggers know about Google page rank and can usually find traffic information and other stuff from Alexa. But few bother to look inside their own blog. If they knew what's happening inside their blog, they would probably be able to manage it better.

What kind of metrics is a blogger looking for?

What makes your blog special? What are visitors looking for on your blog? How long do visitors stay on your blog? Which keywords are best for

Adsense like monetizing tools? These are the basic questions which blog owners must introspect about. This is in addition to information gleamed from other tools and sites like Alexa.

Using Google Analytics

There are numerous tools available on the net, both free and paid to carry out web analytics. But I have found Google analytics is the best. Moreover it is free (you start paying if you are a massive website with thousands of pages). There is another strong reason why I tend to choose Google Analytics. The search market is more or less controlled by Google. The keyword world is Google-centric and this ties up well with your own keyword strategy. This means Google Analytics, keyword analysis, Adwords and Adsense campaigns, all work in tandem. You only have to be smart enough to put the pieces together.

Google Analytics for Blogger and WordPress

There is no way you can escape from the iron grip of Google. Blogger is a great blogging site which belongs to these guys. This means your blog is already optimized for use with Analytics. As regards WordPress, which I suppose is a big player in blogging circles; you need to do a bit to get Analytics to your blog. But it is not difficult. I would consider Analytics critical for your blog's success. You will get to know about things which you never knew earlier. You would be able to find out which posts drive away visitors wand which make them delve further. The bounce rate, as the term is known, can tell you more about your blog than anything else.

What do you do with the Analytics?

The most important function of Analytics is to understand the dynamics of your keywords. You will know which keywords attract most visitors and where they come from. For example, if you submit a guest post to a certain blog, you will immediately be able to find out how many visitors drop into your blog from there. You can then refine your strategy to attract more visitors. Google Analytics is not theory but a solid practical tool. A favorite practice among bloggers is to join forums in social media sites to attract visitors. This is a time consuming process and ultimately you never know if the forum posting generated any traffic. If you add Google Analytics to your blog, you will instantly come to know about the traffic to your site. You can modify your strategy immediately rather than work in the dark.

Knowing what's happening inside your blog and understanding the behavior of visitors is important. This can only happen if you have some analytic tool to assist you. Google Analytics is a fantastic tool for this purpose.

Blogging is actually a simple affair. The requirements are not difficult to understand. Some of the features of a blog are -

Blogging tools

Post: This is where you write your content. Each entry in your blog is called a post. Posts which are dated have to be archived, but still available to visitors. By its very nature a blog is interactive. Readers may have comments to offer which they can enter with the comments link. Lately spamming on comments has become as much of a problem as in emails. Some blogging tools provide anti-spamming facility. Pornographic sites cause maximum disruption. One has to be careful while providing links to other blogs since these links are a source of spam.

Categories: The blogging world moves at a blistering pace. Bloggers want to view other blogs within a tiny time window. This is possible only if one categorizes their posts.

Trackbacks: This is to create a link with other likeminded blogs. The process is automatic and helps communication between two blogs.

Pings: One of the essential differences between a blog and a web-site is the time tracking. Blogs inform other blogs and search engines about their updated status via pinging.

In addition to the above, there are many more definitions and terms. To manage a blog it is not necessary to understand the technology. One need also not be software professional. After all, the purpose of a blog is to air your views. QA number of tools is available for managing your blog. Some of the popular ones are discussed below.

Blogger

Blogger belongs to the Google stable and is free. It has all the features necessary for a blog and one can start blogging within a few minutes. It has attractive templates to choose from and is simple to use. It is highly recommended for first time bloggers.

Typepad

Typepad comes in three flavors, basic, Plus and

Pro. Though the basic version is   stripped down to its bare bones, it is still good enough for first timers who want to get going.

Blogware

This blogging tool is not free. The only feature which differentiates it from others is the FTP feature. This can be quite useful if you want a few static web pages along with your blog.

WordPress

WordPress comes in two flavors. The hosted variety is suitable for newbie's and is quite popular. The software version which comes with the bells and whistles is for the professional blogger.

Movable Type

This is a well known blogging tool. A bit unwieldy for a beginner and requires tweaking.

There are 5 important tools that can help you to analyze your blog. You can know exactly from where you get traffic, how many minutes they've spent on your blog, if they've left any comments, who've read the blog post, etc. These analytics will help you to improve your blog marketing.

Blogs referral sources will tell you from where your traffic through referrals is coming from; whether it is from social media or elsewhere.

Google analytics is the best tool to analyze your blog. It'll give you exact information about your readers.

Etiquette in blogging

We have all heard about etiquette at dinner table, etiquette in business but etiquette in blogging? Why not? Since it is in the public domain and the whole world is going to see it, it is better to follow a code of conduct for blogs. Though blogging is all about expressing yourself freely still there is a certain procedure to follow. One cannot hurt others by blogging. There are certain topics to steer clear off while blogging.

It is better to keep politics and religion out of blogs. This may hurt the religious sentiments of a certain sect of people. Keep your posts updated regularly so that you can look for comments from others if any. Also avoid directly hitting at certain communities as we do not have all the facts related to the incidents. Most of the times, media never gives full information about any untoward incident.

A mother carrying twin baby boys was lamenting in her blog about not having a daughter. This hurt many moms who could not even conceive a baby. So be sensitive to others feelings. Callous comments can hurt people.

While linking your blog to other blogs always ask the other blogger for permission to link with his/her blog. This will earn you respect. Though it is not customary for you to seek permission it is basic courtesy to do so.

Always remember that you are publishing to a world audience. So be accurate about what you are saying. Lies have a way of being discovered. A blogger's reputation is built on   trust and credibility. If one lie is found in your blog, it will destroy all the effort you have put into your blog. There are numerous examples of this happening on the internet.

Another point to note is your language should be good and correct. If there are spellings or grammar errors then people will stop coming to your blog.

The simpler you can keep your content for people to read, the more readers you will attract to your blog. Every person has a different tolerance for spelling problems. You might not mind certain errors, but laugh out loud when you see others. You need to consider that some might consider your own errors in the same manner.

Finally, be yourself and speak with your own voice. Write about how you feel about the issues. Share your insights and feelings on the topics you love. That will draw in people who appreciate your view and who want to hear more. Follow these blogging etiquettes and you will see people rushing to read your blog.

Chapter 9 - Business Blogging

How blogging will help your business

Today media both print and visual have become very expensive to market ones products. Small businesses, consultants and solo entrepreneurs are unable to get due exposure to their product. Blogging gives them the right exposure to prospective customers. Not only can blogs be used for advertising they are also personalized and one to one between the writer and the reader. Blogging establishes brand reputation. How to build a blog which is better than the existing one?

Update your blog regularly. Be truthful and write only about what services you offer. Have great pictures/images about your products which will attract

customers to your site. Retaining clients depends upon how honest you are and how good your service is. A thriving blog can increase traffic, gain confidence with customers and readers amplify your email list and also help you to make money online.

The first thing one need to remember is you don't need to be a 'techie' to start a blog nor an award winning writer. Say for example if you are a travel agent then you can have a blog on places to visit and have links to similar sites and blog posts which offer these services. This way you can boost traffic to your blog post and make money through it as well as improve your business. Make sure that your business blog looks professional and your logo is there on the front page.

A blog is a frequently updated mini-website with special features that makes it easy for readers to comment. All the readers have to do is click on the "comment" link, type in their response, and click "post"...what a great way to hear from your potential clients.

It also organizes each short post you write into categories, providing a 'content management system' so you can easily group all your posts and articles, by sub-topics. Stick to your business plan and focus only on attracting prospective clients. Also remember to update your blog regularly and keep offering freebies for early birds and promotional campaigns improving readers' participation.

Sending newsletters through Emails inviting them to visit your blog is one way of ensuring traffic to your blog. Another method is to write an Ebook and link it to your blog. The Ebook can contain all the information about your business and your blog can update on the information. Once you have your book listed on Amazon it'll create publicity. This has the ability to reach your customers and boost your business quicker than traditional PR means or even email.

Build a better business blog

I suppose if you sell something on your blog it becomes a bu-log or a business blog. But somewhere in the process of selling, the true nature of a blog, which is keeping an informal log of events, is somehow lost. In fact, the difference between blatant selling and subtle suggestion is very thin. A good business blog would not really sell products and services but creatively induce viewers to taste their offering.

The first step towards a business blog or bu-log is to create interest. Take for example a product like infant milk. A good blog would have articles on motherhood and parenting. There would be links to other interesting sites on this subject. A regular post on the do's and don'ts of feeding infants would likely get some viewers attention. At times you should discuss the actual product, its important ingredients. I would promote its protein rich content, Vitamins and minerals essential for a baby. Maybe even a comparison with other products in the same category. All this has to be done in a conversational, easy and informal tone. Hard selling would be a total no-no.

A blog for all practical purposes is a brand on its own. It takes years and years to develop a brand. Building trust and belief in brands is a science by itself; it is the same with a blog. If you imagine that your blog will start producing results in terms of sales within a month, you are in the wrong bu-log. There is a threshold which is required to be crossed. This means a lot of hard work. A business blogger should remember and put all the theory he would have applied to brand building. The blog has to be nurtured and developed. As people come to trust what you say, they will buy what you recommend.

There is one important aspect in business blogging. Never have a payment gateway on your blog. Have a separate site which deals with the actual selling. Your blog should recommend, suggest, hint and cajole viewers to make a purchase. Well designed links dispersed among your blog posts which lead to the product site would be ideal. Don't sell form your Blog. Let people buy off it.

Selling a service with blogging

Blogging provides a worldwide stage for you. Whether you just want to spend some time talking about your daily routine, discuss complex algorithms and mathematical equations, blogs are ideal. But selling a service through your blog is a subtle art which has to be mastered. Hard selling would generally lead to you being shunned by many bloggers. After all, a blog is supposed to be an informal chat room of sorts.

One of the best ways to start selling your services is to create the right atmosphere for it on your blog. For example, if you are an editor or novelist. You just can't start off by saying "Here I am gimme work". You can start off by adding some great posts about editing and writing. Get people interested in your writing. Make it enjoyable, lively, and topical. Let people come to your blog with expectations and go away satisfied. With this kind of wonderful experience, visitors would be receptive to the idea of getting some reviews done by you. Some may have a great story idea which they would like to discuss with you. You have to build credibility among your clientele. Just imagine, you have people coming to your site from all over the world. Your blog is a great opportunity to sell your services and reach out to millions who otherwise would have fallen through the cracks.

If you want to sell your services successfully, you have to participate and give relevant comments on similar blogs. Air your views and actively seek out like minded blogs. More you get to know other bloggers, better the chances of them visiting your blog. Again, be subtle about the services you provide. It is always good to be truthful, honest and clear. Don't brag about yourself. It is likely to put off people.

Create links, links and more links. Ask other bloggers to share a reciprocal link. This would also give you a better ranking on search engines. Just make sure that the links are genuine and related to your subject. Search engines are getting smarter and factor in such issues.

The final word in selling services with blogging is patience. Don't expect people to throng your blog from day one and start purchasing your services immediately. It takes time for a blog to mature and start flowering and giving fruits. Always remember that credibility is important for you and your blog, before anyone buys your services.

Conclusion

You're a blogger or wish to become one, who wanted to know all about blogging and has purchased this ebook. Now that you've read the ebook, take action. Start using all the tips and tricks mentioned in the ebook to make money by promoting your product/ services through blogging. This will not only help in marketing but will also improve your search ranking enabling you to make money through other sources. Remember that where there is a will, there is a way. Be patient, keep watering your plant/ adding content to your blog and one day you'll see beautiful flowers blooming from your plant/ your blog will start earning passive income for you and you'll hear the jingle of money. This is a tried and tested method. Get motivated by the real stories mentioned in the ebook and take action. You'll not only find a way to make money but also an outlet to unleash your talent and creativity. Get going and start blogging....